Voices from Africa and Beyond
A Collection of Poems

Funwi F. Ayuninjam

Langaa Research & Publishing CIG
Mankon, Bamenda

Publisher
Langaa RPCIG
Langaa Research & Publishing Common Initiative Group
P.O. Box 902 Mankon
Bamenda
North West Region
Cameroon
Langaagrp@gmail.com
www.langaa-rpcig.net

Distributed in and outside N. America by African Books Collective
orders@africanbookscollective.com
www.africanbookcollective.com

ISBN: 9956-726-18-4

DISCLAIMER
All views expressed in this publication are those of the author and do
not necessarily reflect the views of Langaa RPCIG.

Table of Contents

III. On The Spiritual

IV. On The Lighter Side

Preface

This collection attempts to capture my sentiments on many plains. Through it, I also take the liberty to capture the sentiments of other persons (either in my life or in society as a whole) as well as the sentiments of other creatures that are part of the chain of life. As a result, much of what follows is occasional poetry, as I have more often than not responded or reacted to my sensations while also being a surrogate for those who could (or would) not express theirs. Having lived abroad for as long as I lived in Cameroon, my perspective has, accordingly, been colored, though not necessarily transmuted. The subdivisions are a matter of convenience only and transcend space and time.

I. ON SOCIETY

Antithetical Planes

During feast days and breaks families
And friends celebrate and bond like allies.
It's occasion for hope and forgiveness
As all is 'bout love, prayer, and saintliness
At the same time, by a single stroke, the judge
Gleefully nullifies many a shameful marriage.

The wealthy man swims in affluence
And a large budget proves his influence.
Many banquets he feels compelled to organize
As he seeks to make the world a paradise.
Yet at the threshold of the party cottage
A Lazarus bows in honor of coinage.

When the baby arrives even with mother's grief,
Many a face sparks with mirth and relief.
Generous gifts from every family and friend
Suggest life and merriment will never end.
But soon comes from afar an elegiac clamor
That's trailed to the churchyard—the peak of honor.

Back to Land

And came the onslaught.
Even those who thought
Little of Ahidjo's politics*
Bowed to his uncanny ethics.

They arrived in the bus loads
From many a crossroads
In South-West's heartland
To the country's hinterland.

Women who had traded with their bodies
Were compelled to try other commodities
To eke out a decent living,
Even if pimps must go starving.

Yes, there was competition in Kumba*
Not for a good cause, but for *njumba*.*
Men would rather be forever boys,
While women chose to be treated as toys.

By ethnic identity they were dispatched,
No matter how well their trade was hatched.
Overnight they had to adopt another trade—
One whose locus the police would need not raid.

Arriving home the women could start over
Without ever needing to take cover.
Some took to farming the wondrous lands;
Others to raising children with husbands.

4

Ahidjo decided to pull the curtain on the drama,
And, thus, ruthlessly ended Kumba's anathema.
It was tough love, no Cameroonian disagreed,
But the only choice by which Kumba would be freed.

* Ahmadou Ahidjo, Cameroon's first post-independence president, was a dictator.
* Kumba: a town in Cameroon's South-West Region
* *njumba*: Cameroon Pidgin English for *prostitute* or *prostitution*

Bartending at the Georgetown Saloun

The apprenticeship was brief: a few hours.
How long to learn the mechanics of a dishwasher?
Pick up plates and glassware from tables?
Clean up after sloppy patrons?
Empty cigarette ashtrays?

It was a popular and busy joint,
The place to be in Georgetown by night—
A live band after nightfall
For people with joie de vivre.
A place for loaded students,
And I was at the serving end.

The rush began at six
And seven saw the music come on.
The hungry fed their faces
And drank their fill and more
In the shaking noise that peaked at one.

Plates filled tables fast
We had to stay with the rush.
Mugs dried up real quick,
And the fish got prompt refills.
The air was thick with smoke
Which had nowhere to go
But toilets with queues of drunks
Waiting to create more room
And stretch the night.
Dames' aprons sagged with notes—
Prizes for glib smiles.

At three we cleaned up
And readied to leave.
"How did it go?" inquired my boss.
"OK," I belied myself.
Of course, tomorrow will usher
A different type of clientele
Or reckon my promotion to management.

The next day I returned
To perfect on Day One.
As the night wore on, my mind kept pace.
My body could take it, not my psyche.
I had made the 3000-mile trip
By choice and by jet,
Not by ship or in shackles.
What would I tell my forebears?
What I despised most
Maybe a dream come true for some Brother.

At what price?

At the end of the night I confessed,
And my boss added up my two nights' worth.

Beware

Beware the snake gliding with grace,
Whose weight on an ant may cause no harm.
It is to zoo-goers often an appealing charm;
Yet when it snaps, its prey needs more than solace.

Beware the pen dripping with many a word
And to the writer is always a willing servant.
It can summon the world for a covenant;
Yet in destruction it surpasses even the sword.

Beware water moving like the impotent,
And even tides cannot hasten its motion.
It beckons us for a dip, also often a passion;
Yet in depth it penetrates as extends the firmament.

Beware the cock crowing in a melodic harmony
And at 1, 3, and dawn reminds the rustic always.
It is the only trustworthy timepiece of his days;
Yet a crow at dusk is the harbinger of tragedy.

Beware the night thickening from shadows
And gives the world a sudden, sullen stillness.
It makes even the brave cower to numbness;

Yet what lurks in it the Almighty alone knows.

Caught Up

I

"Welcome," said the honorable minister,
As I was ushered into the lobby.
Hardly had I nestled into the settee
Than a goblet crashed onto the coffee table
With the tacit offer: Serve what you please!
                    5
An assortment of spirits: Gin, Brandy, Whisky…
Cold though was the feel, the room was refrigerated.
For a while and without budging I stared, undecided.
We traded courtesies as he sipped
Lemon-sprinkled soda through a straw.
                    10
A porter at the door keenly awaited another guest;
A servant paid obsequious attention.
Varnished chairs lined the carpeted balcony.
I grinned and stretched for the Whisky:
My left foot stamped onto the immense floor
                    15
And sank ankle deep into the spongy carpet.
The endless walls, like the tables, shone with tiles
And bore the label ABSOLUTELY NO SMOKING.
"How's school," inquired His Excellency.
My response blended with the usher of a business guest.

20

As I sipped I thought I heard the *mbaya**
Shattering the quiet of the neighborhood.
Then my eyes settled on a gold-plated discographer,
Below which was a steel pendulum now chiming six.

25

When I stepped outside,
Backed the paragon of masonry,
And began to breathe again
The fresh air of the careless world,
I thought I had been in Dreamland.

II

30

Pa Wandah's hut was warm and welcoming.
It stood out in its own right within the hamlet.
I found my seat—a wooden lion engraving.
The old man puffed smoke carelessly off his pipe
While the cheerful fire burned ceaselessly.

35

The adobe walls, for ages bathed in smoke,
Glittered with soot…like flattened eggshells.
Surrounding him were infants
Relishing the comfort of the smoke…
Little foreheads swollen with folktales

40

How many the gods alone know.
He wobbled off and brought back a horn
Which I took with a slight forward jerk.
He filled it with warm raffia palm-wine.
"How far have you gone with book?"

45
"I have just started big book," I said.
He asked about my health and my family.
Then like father to son:
"Let no girl fool you...her real want is money."
The children's voices were drowned by ours
50
As they stole speech only by fidgeting.
The modulating sound of the town-crier
Alerted the entire village
It was moonlight enough
For the night masqueraders to start readying.
55
I emptied my fifth horn standing.
"Be careful stepping out," cautioned he.
"Greet your mother and your siblings."
Striding outward I disliked the cold air
And wished I could have remained;
60
I really wished time had a turning.

* *Mbaya*: a Cameroonian dance of Nso origin

Christmas in Cameroon

I miss the zest: fresh haircuts, new shoes, colorful clothes;
The morning chill and dusty roads that no one loathes;
The sweet smell of smoke from the farm compost—
The only daytime oven that a mother may ever boast.

I miss the fresh, bowing roadside elephant-grass stems
Which at youth were to unwilling vegetarians gems;
The whistling pine needles and the ripening bananas;
The humming wind rushing leaves under verandahs.

I miss the dew that laminates the ice-cold grass
As we stream to church for Christmas morning mass,
The stillness and peace of the wondrous sky far above
That beckon feuding families 'n pals to talk with love.

I miss the serenity of service and the angelic singing,
The day-long merrymaking: eating, drinking, dancing,
The awe, fright, and sprite of the tireless, jocular juju
Which, for tips, makes Christmas Day a week or two.

I miss the savory smell of evening dew and lovely sunset—
Reminders of the approaching end to the day's banquet.
It's time for revelers and guests to start heading home
Before deep darkness takes over the heavenly dome.

I miss the easy, benign spirit of the short season
Which, even for business minds, is no reason
To make families 'n partygoers overpay
To relish the wistful smell of Christmas Day.

Distant though I've been in space and time
From my early adulthood through my prime,
I've drawn from the memories once each year
With the approach of Christmas, a season so dear.

Customs Inspection in Douala

She greeted me with a toothy smile
As I stepped forward with my cargo.
With my four valises on the conveyor belt,
The glow turned to excitement only I would melt.

Her khaki still spotless and well pressed;
Her cap neat and well sat.
Unduly courteous she was;
Crisp and impressionable was her French.

"How far have you come?"
Lest I try to fool her,
She looked at my luggage tags and blurted, "*Etats-Unis!*"
Then opened the first piece and combed it with interest.
"Why so much luggage?"
"I have a large family" (no place for non-cooperation)

She zipped back the valise, marked it, and opened the next.
"Où est pour moi?" she asked, beaming.
Unconvinced I had heard her right,
I begged for clarification.
She meant it: "*Where is mine?*"
Matter-of-factly I regretted
Mine was home—a large family
And to everyone a tangible handshake at arrival.

Half-way through the third valise,
She pressed, only threateningly—
"You can see the labels," I said innocently.

Her disenchantment discernible
"You may have to declare all the contents."
Her junior colleagues gestured me for US green backs.
She had me follow her eyes to her shoulder strap: two stars
I still would not settle.

Suddenly, the inspector would rather not inspect
And ordered the checked luggage placed back
On the conveyor belt, in reverse.
"Take it downstairs to the commissioner."
Her tone was terse and definite.
"Next!"

Also resolute was I.
"You must come with me and explain *'Où est pour moi?'*"
Frozen, she yielded…
And the last piece escaped inspection.

Ecstasy at a Washington Joint

As the sun lavishly unleashed
Its heavenly curse of heat that Sabbath day,
Two ill-fated scalawags in dripping jeans
Scampered behind two spices of life.
Soon after the women nosed their luck
In flight they turned around towards the clients—
Each party anxious for different motives.
Thus began the transaction.

What women!
The one skeletal and famished,
With an index finger grating her merchandise.
She whetted the man's appetite for germs.
The other pudgy, and for underwear
Lumps of protoplasm on either side of her loin,
Both shields protruding sharply and trailing her.
Her chest carrying ten-pound sloppy yams

And the angels
Split between a second's ecstasy
And a week's rent and groceries
And worse
Looked at the "P" Street commuters unabashedly.
Who cares?
One couple struck a deal;
Money changed hands
And towards an apartment complex
At Fourteenth 'n "P" they swaggered.
Behind a long-forgotten car in a garage the maniacs

Under the blazing sun pulled down.

Two belles,
Unwishing the sight,
Started off, albeit secretly spying back.
And it was all over.
The ecstasy, not the unquenchable thirst,
As the deal had punctured his wallet.
He came off half-frowning, not she…
Beaming and adjusting her innerwear
With her left index finger
And leading her fellow Eve to a 7-Eleven,
Whence they re-emerged with cups of soda
Which they gulped down.

Nausea

Suddenly
That mid-summer afternoon
All eyes followed her.

She looked charming in summer shorts
Lipstick covered a pair of dimples
She beamed as her hair shuffled in the wind,
Infant leaning on the quintessence of beauty.

When the 42 DC Metro bus stopped,
They stood up to go, child first.

Then
Along her back thighs
All the way to her ankles
Trailed two pink bubbles.

And then
Another six-year-old
Looked at her mom imploringly.

Trumpet Blast

The trumpet blast,
Once a call to teatime teens,
Now leads the funeral convoy
And summons the hungry,
Summons the thirsty,
Summons the traders,
Summons the hungry, the thirsty…

The deceased passes into oblivion
And awaits the kind, patient embrace
Of Mother Earth…of ravenous worms.

For days the grief stricken,
With tears rolling down,
Are overshadowed by food, by drinks
And want
Of more food, more drinks
Till the barns and cellars empty…
Till another trumpet blast.

II.   ON KITH AND KIN

Another Word: From Father to Daughter

It was, it seems, only yesteryear
We could not wait another year
Till, without help, you could bear
Yourself without making us fear.

And, oh! how sweet the sacrifice,
Fond the memories, which bear no price.
Yes, oblivious you were of today's malice,
And spongy was your mind for our advice.

Now you're more than Diane, our Princess;
Almost overnight your steady progress
Into adulthood is measured much less
In physique and gait than in finesse.

Beware, beware of your doting peers
And all whom you may call your dears.
Even if to you they give three cheers,
For them will be their first and last fears.

Give only to a select few your trust,
For many a lad will see you only with lust.
If need be have them bite the dust.
Listen to your mind (not your heart) as a must.

You have often heard Mommy and me
Tell you how good a girl you must be.
Sooner or later you must make us see
You truly are your own self, Princess D.

The choices are all yours to make—
Not for us but for your self, your sake.
You have a dream to live, a life to make
But perverts you must eye to forsake.

Although today's choices may seem sure,
Tomorrow they'll look no less than poor.
Therefore, think and think some more
Before you let Ruin knock on your door.

Home

I have nurtured many an ambition
From youth to this noon of age;
Have sought to fly ever higher
But, too, further and further away
From the threshold, the source
Only to find that home is the best place.

I have always remembered my Old Man
And deeply pitied my pining, wearied mother,
And in my troublous life, yet unstoppable pursuit,
Hoped one day to show my gratitude to both,
But the further I search, the more I feel (un)wanted
Because home is the best place.

At the U.S. Marine Corps War Memorial
With throngs of visitors I relished the early spring air
And for a minute was lost:
A sea of tourists with kites and balloons hovering
Every space full: the lawns, the sidewalks, the air.
There, before my eyes, was D.C. throbbing with life.

Back in my room I thought I had run a marathon.
I could see and feel from across the window
The rare friendly budding flowers, harbinger of spring.
Could only see and smell but dare not touch them!
Doubtless we were friends, but friends apart
And then suddenly came surging thoughts of home.

Everyone says "Hi" and lavishes giggles;

Everyone is friendly without being a friend.
The sunlit panorama is charming and inviting,
But under the moonlight, horror and death abound.
No reminder to do nothing where I have nothing to do,
So the inner voice persists, "Home is the best place."

A Sudden End

For a moment I was unconvinced, dazed
As I looked at happy shoppers streaming by;
Aware of my shrunken world…not even a goodbye?
We headed back to his ward. I was amazed.

Mr. Niba had given me a firm handshake
And a reassuring look that said it all:
Papa has answered the ultimate call.
Fear not…none of you shall we forsake.

He had left for Bamenda General Hospital
On his own accord just the day before
With only a handbag, hoping for nothing more
Than a doctor's visit…a routine physical.

But there he lay—soft, smiling, but lifeless;
Unresponsive to our cries and hopeless calls.
Sure, there were mocking echoes from the walls.
Could the Almighty also be this merciless?

The following day Papa was reason
For a ten-mile procession to a celebration
Not of the fulfillment of an ambition
Or the rich harvest of the rainy season.

He was laid to rest at home—in the backyard
By Grandma Meba'atu…not by church convention,
Because, for the holy, he was not a Christian
Deserving of God's sacred, venerable orchard.

Where might he be now? I sometimes ponder:
In hell-fire as Cameroon's Catholics hold?
Ha! Ha! Perhaps an assumption too bold!
Why not in the warm bosom of his mother?

Could son and mother both be bound in hell?
Long as I see Papa sharing in my ecstasy
Or guiding me through every quandary,
Hell will for me remain a hard sell.

Not hell if he is in the joyful company
Of his father, mother, other forebears –
People of whom he nursed no fears,
And with whom he now shares a destiny.

If there be any eternal blaze,
It's one that forever kindles
Family spirits for tales and riddles
That convey history in a maze.

Michael's Last Days

He was vivacious and fun loving,
Physically fit and hard working;
Hopeful for a liberal-arts education
But settled for a practical vocation.

Michael's was a life full of promise:
College and a career in the civil service—
A chance to return his parents' sacrifices,
But a vile monster lurked on the premises.

In his head was a most cowardly predator
Waiting for him like a lender a debtor.
The diagnosis was sobering: a brain tumor,
Which ended all we shared, starting with humor.

Schooling soon ground to a screeching halt,
And "A"s became blanks…none of his fault.
Doctors scrambled daily for an explanation
But gave only hope as we prayed for remission.

Months later it became quite evident
Mighty T had made a big-enough dent
Into Michael's body and yielding psyche
And recovery was a near-impossibility.

He was discharged from Bamenda General
As the prognosis became even more dismal.
For weeks he groaned and moaned nightly,
Calling for help from Francis and Anthony.

We were solicitous but just as helpless;
Our prayers and succor seemed bootless.
What else could we do, I daily lamented.
Of all, the late diagnosis I most regretted.

And then it all ended: God's will fulfilled?
Do we say Michael suffered for having defiled
God's virtue from which there was no redemption?
Or might he for survivors be a mere illustration?

To everyone, young and old, an earned last day
Over which even modern medicine has no say.
But oh how sweet it'd be if God gave an excuse
To melt the tears of mourners who the call refuse.

Mother

Magnanimous towards the weak and helpless
Optimistic about a tomorrow without Pain
Tolerant of other views about spirituality
Hopeful for a better world for womankind
Eager to learn from us even as you aged
Resourceful in providing for us without reserve

Modest in material wishes and expecting little
Open-minded about the world beyond
Thankful for grand- and great-grandchildren
Humble in accepting the Lord's burden
Engaging in recounting times long past
Reassuring of the possibilities, be they illusive

The Last Conversation

The request was urgent, the message clear:
Drop everything and come back home Dear.
My health is steadily deteriorating,
My physical energies fast waning.

I found her in good spirits, full of wit
And wondered if the summon had merit.
But a different feeling she had
As may never be known to a lad.

My sun is fast setting, said she,
And further suffering I need not see.
Seek to level with each other always
For infighting or slander never pays.

She disclosed her fiscal wealth and missives
And gave me advanced directives.
Numbed and befuddled was I
As her testament I could not decry.

When I left I promised to action
Her repeated request to bring the children.
No response…had heard it before.
Weeks later I got the call: she was no more.

Mother: A Farewell

You took up the mantle upon Papa's passing
And for 33 years bore it, barely complaining;
Yet all you asked of me lately: to bring the children
I so delayed they will come home only to brethren.

I regret not being there to help dispel Pain,
But admire your will to tell her "shame" again.
Alas, there'll be no Christmas visit with you,
But the children's memories of times past will do.

I know from yonder you still can hear me:
What you've asked of me will come to be.
Your humility and grace will for me remain
A legacy always to cherish and maintain.

Although you had your share of earthly strife,
Yours was a simple, prayerful, dignified life.
If heaven is indeed a place of peaceful rest,
You are already there as God's timeless guest.

Visiting the Grave of Mami Rebecca

She passed away in December Nineteen-Eighty.
I'd returned on break, having celebrated three and twenty.
I was in disbelief when I learned about it:
A lonely, shameful finale by all counts unfit
For a woman with many adult children
And a throng of successful lawyer brethren.

She was found next morn on her adobe verandah
Weather beaten, hands clasped pointing to Allah.
To spite my family, hers chose to bury
Her on my father's business property.
All squabbles about land being devalued
Were dwarfed by talk of my family being sued.

All temporal matters I quickly set aside
As I went to the grave and stood alongside
The mound and peered at the headstone –
Reflecting on Mami Rebecca in prayerful tone.
I returned home and to everyone reported
My visit and proximity to the departed.

I had, thus, sparked another potential tragedy...
For that compound was anathema to my family.
My mother rushed me to a native doctor,
Who prepared some portions to counter
A poison that had been buried on the grounds
To trap us, should we dare to go out of bounds.

Certain I was of my own looming, inevitable end.

With the last days *in* sight, an epitaph I penned:

The cock has crowed, but I am yet to snooze.
The moon is up, but my spirits are low;
Harvest time is near, but I am yet to sow;
The wine gourd is empty, but I am yet to booze.

The sun is down, but I am yet to rise;
The feast is over, but I am yet to have a seat.
Long is the road, but sore are my feet;
The race is over, but I have won no prize.

The wedding day is near, but where is the groom?
The coal is turning ash, but why is the house still cold?
My time is up, but when shall I do something bold?
Let it be! Ask the ancestors, not the seers of doom.

Three decades later I still live to ponder:
WHY? Only the ancestors can answer.

III. On The Spiritual

Almighty God

Almighty God,
Thou have endowed humanity with intellect
And strength to work together…
A co-mingling of desires worth the gaze
Of both the sane and the lunatic.
But all this race is an entity
That, like the pendulum, swings freely.

Almighty God,
Thou have created a faculty of thought
That seeks to perfect its every art
As does the cicada its love song.
Man's artistry inspires even the mad with awe.
But all these quests are like the job of the well-digger
Who, unchecked, might be hollowing his casket.

Almighty God,
Thou have made a universe
Of unequalled adornment,
Of a variety to be sung by the king fisher.
But are these imaginations,
Like the wind vane during a storm,
Spinning harum-scarum?

Creation's Might

Vegetation that at times defies the drought
And gives the world a marveling beauty
Is life's first guarantor of survival.
But when the harmattan starts whistling
And dryness descends upon the earth,
And skyscrapers have to surface,
Vegetation shrinks helplessly to death.

The hills and mountains that go buried
As up the heavens they soar
Are solid, timeless windbreaks.
But when the bulldozers roar
And set on carving a new road,
And tunnels are in the blueprint,
Mountains, like Moses's Red Sea, cleave.

Man, patron of God's marvels
And peerless in intellect and talent
Is also the earthly Almighty.
But when Death feigns discontent
And Age feigns unequalled pride,
And Illness has to bear Death's desire,
Man, like an evening primrose, shrivels.

Even rhyme that conserves thought and feeling
And helps retrieve man's fleeting memories,
Is the most perfect trustee of Learning.
But when Mars casts his pestilent glimpse
And to the roundtable concord says No!

And archives have to come crashing down,
Rhyme, like bursting balloon air, vanishes.

But, thank goodness, not all will die:
When woodlands, foliage, pastures...all plant life
In the face of drought and masonry wrinkle and droop;
Schools, archives, landscape, and animal life
Fall prey to industry and armed conflict,
The world, as the Second Day,
Remains air, water, and earth invincible.

Dawn at Dusk

She had been a patient spinster
Far longer than most live with a sir.
But just as she began to wonder
If the sun would ever shine on her,
Came an eager golden-year starter.

Without warning the sky turned gray
And like a peevish baby shed tears
On bewildered plowmen just starting their day.
The sudden turn was unknown even to seers.
As the team turned tail, a rainbow saved the day.

She had toasted at many a birthday shower
To hail every friend's 'n neighbor's new arrival,
Though no child would likely ever call her mother.
As her sun began to set, she reckoned her fate final.
But, like Elizabeth,* learned she would be a mother.

She was rounding up on a full century
And, as a widow, had seen life's every pitfall
And her fair share of strife and penury.
All she longed for was the final call.
As night fell she could see her ancestry.

---

* Elizabeth, Zechariah's wife, was barren till her old age, when she became pregnant with the future John the Baptist.

Humility

Confronted with a defying position,
All conceit and pomp quickly diminish,
And, like a supplicant at confession,
You crumble as if you have lived your wish.
To the sodden brain no longer knowing his way
Wholesome concern you readily lavish.
A pin-drop suffices to diminish
Pleasure and invite all concern your way.
An artless toddler would to the fullest
Entertain with matter of no interest;
The coo-coo to the mind searching silence
Restores that which now functions without pretence.
 Thus, all will-power and physique fast yield
 To stress that takes composure far afield.

Illness

Illness, you wrap the firm body with grief
And health from the strong you fast diminish.
Dethroning his spirit to live his wish,
You crown yourself and then heave in relief.
When inoculations cause but distress
And the body cells to you quickly yield,
Joy takes your heart as do locusts the field,
While a man you gently command armless.
But when physics 'pon you comes to nothing,
And the patient one final time yelps "Hm,"
And the gong tolls for final rites at home

That a procession leads to – inurning,
  Illness, too, is lowered into the grave
  And will not rise without facing the brave.

Peace I

At youth, when innocence is cognition,
All is logic and glee is without end.
Body and soul are lax in temptation
And to youths life should never know an end.
Grown, snag upon snag weighs down the physique.
The mind many a tempting risk harbors,
Which drain the soul of rest and make it sick—
Rendering a youth with vigor a life corpse.
But in want of gone pleasure and extra,
Distraction and good company are sought:
Clubs, sports, outings, festivals, et cetera.
One is alive, be it only in thought.
  Yet when the calm of solitude descends,
  Back come all fears that life adds to nerve ends.

Peace II

When the fetus is forced out in a painful blast,
Many decades it has to suffer life's torments;
His are fragmentary and wearisome moments,
And, till earth retakes him, it's been a grueling past.
When the testa explodes, freeing both shoot and root,
Preying animals, birds, and insects on it count.
Not till they've played their part and joined earth in one mount
Do they enjoy the peace of decay—time's output.
When the spring a powerful wriggle unleashes,
Many a change still lies before the endless worm.
Immortal rocks and waves a powerful front form.
Not till it joins the deadly sea is there stillness.
    After a restive life comes immutable calm;
    Free from time's sway, life is complete with death's balm.

Sin

None ever since the Transgression has proved more vain
Than you, shamed Sin, haunting ghost of forlorn Satan,
Since that cursed day on woman you tested your brain
To turn mankind into mortals thanks to Woman.
Where are you, or where are you not, to dwell, foul Sin?
In bars, theaters, and chapels you are a quick find.
Shall the soul no longer age with virtue therein?
Must your strength seek to propel blemishes in mankind?
Though a potential occupant of man's weak soul,
You surely cannot stake so great a claim on strength,
For the penitent, bent on turning from your foul,

Needs only say the Act of Contrition at length
  Or hurry to the priest's bar for your betrayal,
  And in seconds he's free and once more God's loyal.

Sleep

Sleep, after a day's restless discharges,
Keeps my body calm and my soul at peace.
To stretch sleep and lend more mental release,
I take to poppies, which too drown worries.
Thus, like youths on Christmas seats, I mistake
Time has no turning, nor feasting an end.
But oftentimes sleep and rest only rend—
Driving the soul on horrid trips sans stake
And inviting thoughts which don't belong,
Which haunt my soul all night and all day long.
Who filches from me my good sleep robs me
Of what doesn't enrich him; yet drains me.
  Alas, worries remain invincible—
  Being nowhere in the world invisible.

IV. ON THE LIGHTER SIDE

Broken Romance

Glued onto each other,
two cockroaches,
out of a hideout,
dared into a North-West D.C. street.

First with an air of contempt,
and then with one of despair,
with a vicious stamp I uncoupled them
and each its way scrammed for life.

One to the loveseat returned;
the other, amidst the commotion
and still in half-joy pants,
dashed into the mid-lane--a world away from Madame.

But realizing his folly,
and sensing the chance of a lonesome night,
he quickly brought to a halt his senseless flight
and declared war on the transgressor at his threshold

With an insect I fought,
and with it I would lose face
at Morgan-'n-Fourteenth
before bewildered lookers-on.

As my face glared with sweat
and my foe was dead set
on resuming the broken romance,
my jealousy turned to frustration.

With the bitter joy of truth,
I conceded.
Is *eunuch* now only a word
or still also organic?

From Lord to Lady

A strange peace and quietude
This evening gently envelop me.
A soul for long hours and days without end
Besieged and ravished by psychic fog
Will from this moment through eternity
Be battered and possessed by a Seraph
Three thousand miles from Washington.

Let metaphysics upon this
Be dulled to its ebb of ebbs;
Let telephone friends fall fated tears
Of eavesdroppers as I keep saying, "Hold the line"
While sceptered kings, like perched hawks,
Descend and endow us both with their majesties,
For psychic bliss can be a measure of wealth.

Let my amoebic, insatiable zest of old
In whatever minds recall patent neglect;
My unimpeachable veer close behind the Glow
Sages and longing, lingering looks disapproves.
Summon tens of Pilates, bedeviling spirits
Unto my bench and I'll be rid of all my pardons.
    For I need peace and quietude no more;
    For I've been seeking incognito this lone threshold.

Happy Birthday (to Gisèle)

The clocks chimed midnight
And quickly ushered the world
Into Friday, July Fourth, Eighty.
But you particularly passed
Into the Seventeenth –
So your heart leapt with the time
That meant all for you.
Ahead lie dinners and cocktails,
Wishes from loved ones
And tokens from sweethearts
To share a great day.
Today you unsheathe yourself
As you enter your Seventeenth
To receive the benediction of Venus,
Which will not with dusk perish
But will forever with you abide.
As your limbs grow and flesh deepens,
So too should your mind and senses broaden
So at noon you will find yourself
Regretless, fully on the beat.
Now muse:

Oh ever-ready Venus, teach me
To open my heart where's no deceit,
To smile where I'll be answered,
To kiss where's no sting
To know voices that will reckon my birth hereafter.

As Birthday Seventeen crows forth, loving Father,
Give me an immaculate heart –
That I may smile truly to friends;
An invulnerable spirit –
That friendships never must flee;
A most charitable heart –
That love, before lust, can share in sentiments;
A good sense of judgment –
That I may show justice to my world;
Patience and forgiveness –
That I can be an example;
Knowledge and wisdom –
That I may be a good shepherd;
This double thread of my life –
That I may never be surprised.

If Time Can Heal

You touched my heart and left
With nothing to show for the cleft.
I couldn't tell you you truly did,
So sealed my grief beneath a lid.

You gave me the first kiss,
Primed me for romantic bliss,
And fast became my only pride
As all Valentines I tossed aside.

Oh but how Space kills!
Her force was beyond the pills
As she stole my heart overnight,
And I caved even without a fight.

As you moved on, so did I
Sure you couldn't hurt even a fly.
To throngs I became a rainbow—
To relish from afar, but to touch…oh no!

To you I closed the door to my heart,
Certain I had played my part.
What Space and Time took away
Mem'ries replenished by the day.

Tears? All dried up by cheers
Of envious friends and four dears
Who helped to quench my passionate flames
With what was only mental games.

Though fully content with my stead,
My loss my heart continues to dread.
Though nothing can reverse your choice,
I will remember your soft voice.

Looking Forward

As we look to the end of the day
So to work and school and more we may say
Hasta manana! Work has no end.
Yet surely we inch towards year's end.

As we look to the end of the week
For more fun and rest to seek
We come ever closer to emptying
Our purses with little warning.

As we look to the next paycheck
We bemoan our loose spending break
But with each tax contribution
We near retirement obligation.

As we look to another birthday
With pomp we mean to honor and pay
Tribute to Youthfulness and Zest—
Age's yearly nemesis at best.

Be it the end of day, week, month, year
We embrace with joy what we most fear
And so, tick by tick, incognito
We advance into sunset and limbo.

Mosquito and Ear

When still youthful and thought he was onto glory,
Mosquito to Ear sauntered and proposed with surety.
Whether it was by high design or mere jesting,
Ear, without any delay, shuck Mosquito off, saying,
"With these limbs of yours, how many days more
Ere the neighborhood urgently gathers before
Your yard to honor your wretched limbs in songs of praise?"
Thus addressed, the suitor sank and for days
Not a word between them was transmitted.
Mosquito, who was known to be conceited,
And so meant to remain, to Ear strode and said smiling,
"To you I came certain I was only deigning,
But your answer testifies to a poor taste of elegance,
And for that I shall chastise you with my absence."
Thus said, Mosquito walked off without delay.
While Ear, holding her head, swaggered off her own way.
But that's not the entire tale as it's to folklore known.
For Mosquito, to spite unbending, thus set it down:
To assert my vitality, I will henceforth call at Ear's,
And do so very frequently through the years.

Romance and Divinity

My graceful love,
Upon you I bestow my looks,
And so inquire:
What sport tonight?
        Dearest in Christ,
        The curfew tolls six
        And, this rosary in hand,
        I beseech thee: Seek God's mercy.

My lone dream,
Upon thee I lavish hope,
And unto those stainless cheeks
Dare I lay my duty?
        Oh! Loving brother,
        It's time for evening care
        And kids at home
        Await evening grace.

My eyes, my only light,
Onto thy sole hand
I commend my life
For you to man henceforth.
        Fellow believer in the Trinity,
        With you may I commiserate
        On a love that's but frosty?
        Another choice I exhort you to make.

The breezy daffodils on the lakeshore
Invite couples to waddle hand in hand

Fully awake to the call of nature.
And also waken to the call of Venus!
  Ay! To His nature, I see.
  These daffodils…life in Christ
  Now call on the beatitudes
  And an ample following there is.

But I prefer that tonight
We dance ourselves to a crib,
And all madly conceived reveries
You set aside for the morrow!
  Oh! Now I seem
  To hear you no more clearly
  Than does a babe a popinjay
  When high upon his honor.

Visit with Me Tonight

As I close my eyes tonight
I can see your delightful fog
Descending on me, binding me, cuddling me
Answering my call to visit with me tonight

And soon I can feel
The ever so gentle, ever soothing fingers
All over me…just where they belong
Caressing, smoothing, stroking…

Our heartbeats, our minds in soulful sensual sync
As we relish a mineral bath in a celestial spring
With the waves lapping up ashore…
From smooth 'n gentle to wild 'n crazy
From east to west 'n north to south
Throughout this visit with me tonight

And we ready to tango again
Going from east to west 'n north to south
With our eyes fully fastened through the small hours

The Spider and the Housefly

One warm afternoon a bulky housefly,
Lax in spirit, went out the yard to spy.
Sprouting freely around a white ceiling
He saw no rival and thought he was everything.
As Spider crawled past the healthy youngster,
The promenade quickly turned Fly into a hunter.
As Almighty of the ceiling universe, Fly laid
Eyes on Spider and fast decided on a raid.
He was within proximity and too silly
To awaken a spirit rarely saintly.
Gentle Spider, not eager for the fray,
Took a different turn, as a cat at play.

But now thrice, and with cause, Spider lost his temper.
"What's a fly's business these days with a spider?"
He pondered, his heart now thumping.
"I'll stop and wait; my fear isn't the ring!"
Fly crept forth steadily, with the audacity of right
In hope his *prey* shouldn't again take flight.

In a split-second the two were face to face,
And here was for both the end of the race.
Fly made the first dash at the meaty bait;
Spider rather contemplated his foe's fate.
Now too close to escape, Fly saw his folly
As his *prey's* muscle emerged wholly.
In an attempt to escape, be it to no avail,
Fly wailed helplessly and tried to turn tail.
Like long-lost pals in happy reunion,

Spider grabbed Fly, but proceeded to mastication.

As Fly from his own folly couldn't learn,
Let this to the fly world be a thing to spurn:
Getting into a fight without assurance
Of your opponent's esteem and endurance.